BUILDINGS AT WORK

Hospitals

ELIZABETH ENCARNACION

QED Publishing

First published in the UK in 2007 by
QED Publishing
A Quarto Group company
226 City Road
London EC1V 2TT
www.qed-publishing.co.uk

A catalogue record for this book is available from the British Library.

ISBN 978 1 84538 674 0

Written by Elizabeth Encarnacion
Designed by Rahul Dhiman (Q2A Media)
Series Editor Honor Head
Foldout illustration by Ian Naylor
Picture Researcher Sujatha Menon

Publisher Steve Evans
Creative Director Zeta Davies
Senior Editor Hannah Ray

Printed and bound in China

Picture credits
Key: T = top, B = bottom, C = centre, L = left, R = right, FC = front cover

Science Photo Library/ Photolibrary: 4–5 (background), 7m, 13t, 13b, 15t, 16–17 (background), 18, 23t, 32, **Bsip/ Photolibrary**: 6–7 (background), 8b, 14, 15m, CHEN WEI SENG/ **Shutterstock**: 6b, Nruboc **Dreamstime.com**: 8–9 (background), **Photo Researchers, Inc./ Photolibrary**: 9t, 12b, 25m, iceninephoto/ **Istockphoto**: 10b, **Picture Press/ Photolibrary**: 11, **Phototake Inc/ Photolibrary**: 17t, **Index Stock Imagery/ Photolibrary**: 17b, Cliff Hollis, ECU News and Communication Services: 21, **Photonica Inc/ Photolibrary**: 23b, Louisiana State University: 24–25 (background), Y-12 National Security Council: 24b, **navy.mil**: 26–27 (background), Tim Fisher; **The Military Picture Library/Corbis**: 27t, **Mass Communication Specialist 2nd Class Timothy F. Sosa./ navy.mil**: 27m, Carolinas Med- 1/ Metropolitan Medical Response System: 28–29 (background), 29t, Joao Luiz Bulcao/**Corbis**: 29b, muc-spotter.de/ **Jetphotos.net**: 31t, Graber AG, Switzerland: 33t, Israel Sun Ltd./ **Foreign Press Services**: 33b.

Words in bold can be found in the Glossary on page 34.

CONTENTS

Hospitals 4

Clinics 6

General hospitals 8

Emergency centres 10

Teaching hospitals 12

Maternity units 14

Operating theatres 16

Specialized hospitals 22

Field hospitals 24

Hospital ships 26

Hospitals on wheels 28

Air ambulances 30

Animal hospitals 32

Glossary 34

Find out more 35

Index 36

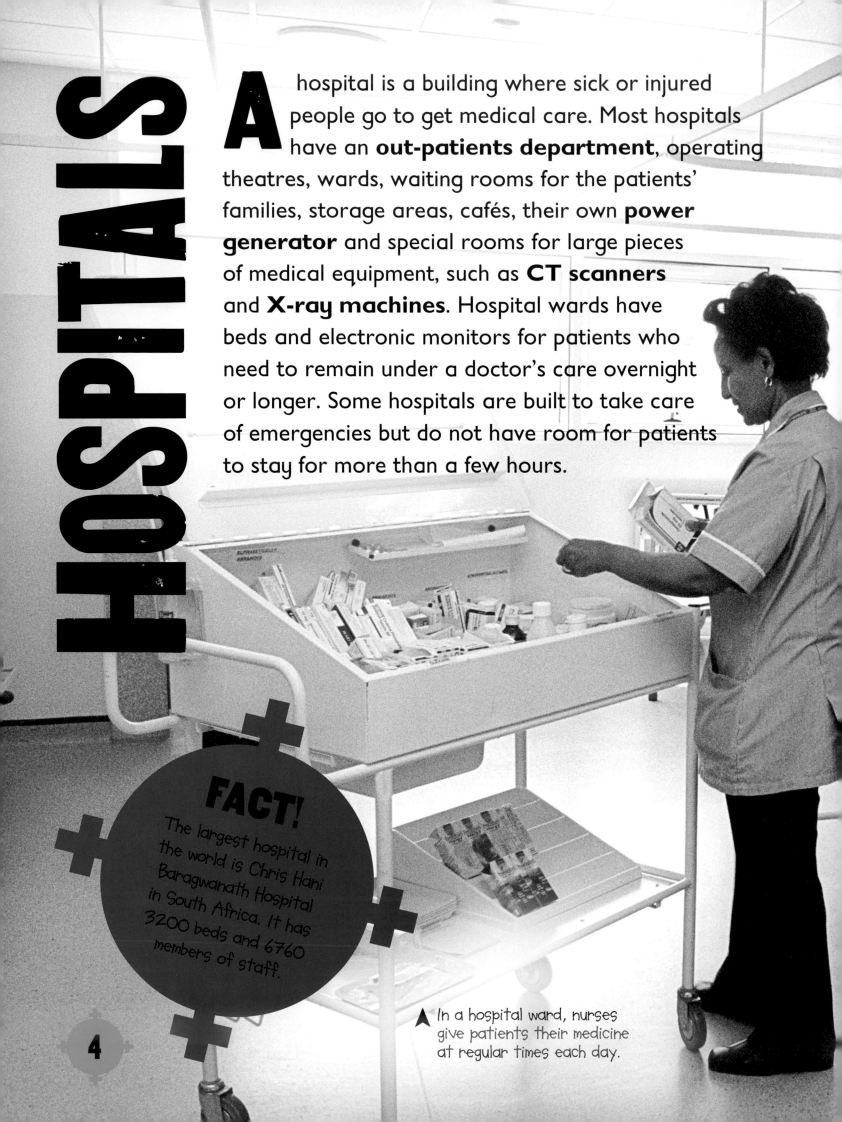

HOSPITALS

A hospital is a building where sick or injured people go to get medical care. Most hospitals have an **out-patients department**, operating theatres, wards, waiting rooms for the patients' families, storage areas, cafés, their own **power generator** and special rooms for large pieces of medical equipment, such as **CT scanners** and **X-ray machines**. Hospital wards have beds and electronic monitors for patients who need to remain under a doctor's care overnight or longer. Some hospitals are built to take care of emergencies but do not have room for patients to stay for more than a few hours.

FACT!
The largest hospital in the world is Chris Hani Baragwanath Hospital in South Africa. It has 3200 beds and 6760 members of staff.

In a hospital ward, nurses give patients their medicine at regular times each day.

4

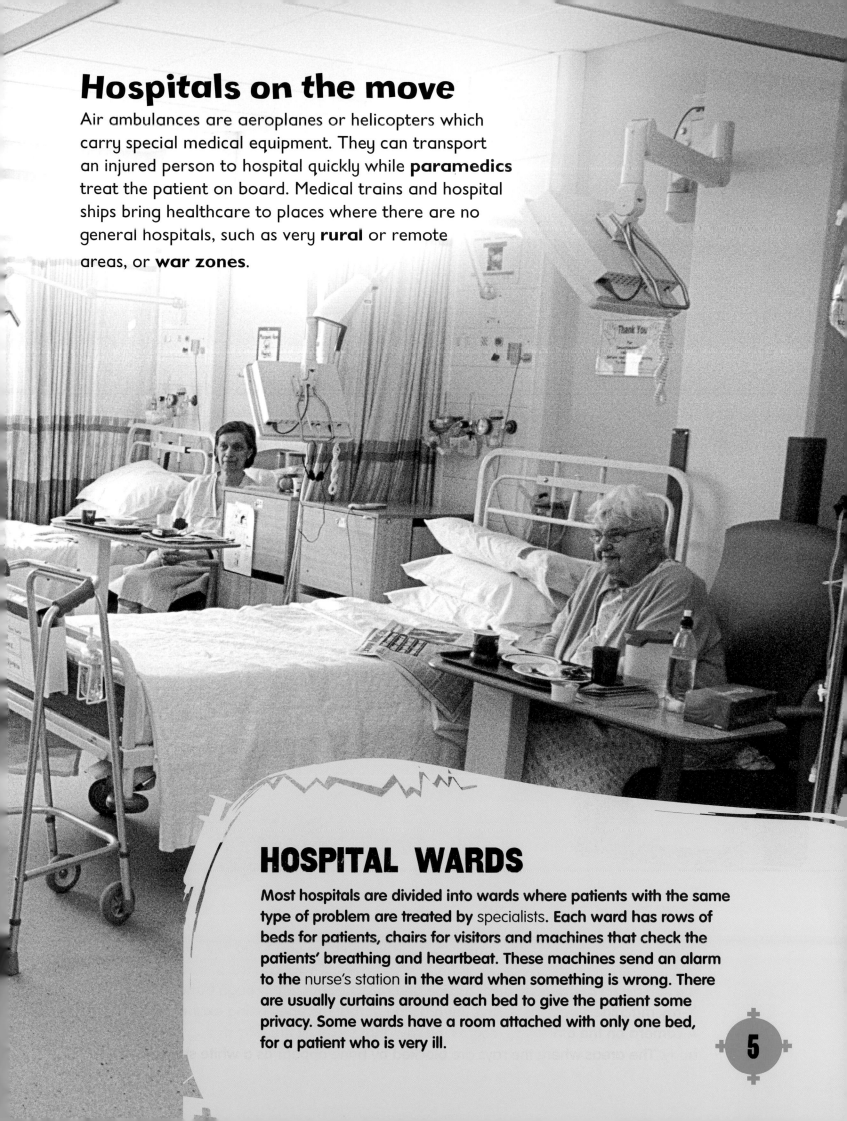

Hospitals on the move

Air ambulances are aeroplanes or helicopters which carry special medical equipment. They can transport an injured person to hospital quickly while **paramedics** treat the patient on board. Medical trains and hospital ships bring healthcare to places where there are no general hospitals, such as very **rural** or remote areas, or **war zones**.

HOSPITAL WARDS

Most hospitals are divided into wards where patients with the same type of problem are treated by specialists. Each ward has rows of beds for patients, chairs for visitors and machines that check the patients' breathing and heartbeat. These machines send an alarm to the nurse's station in the ward when something is wrong. There are usually curtains around each bed to give the patient some privacy. Some wards have a room attached with only one bed, for a patient who is very ill.

CLINICS

A clinic or a doctors' surgery is a medical centre that offers basic health care, such as yearly checkups, **antenatal care** and treatment for mild illnesses such as a throat infection. Clinics are usually for people whose injuries or illnesses are not bad enough for them to go to a general hospital. Clinics have a waiting area, with chairs and magazines for patients who are waiting to be seen by a doctor. Many clinics also have a pharmacy – a place where a patient can get their medicine once they have seen a doctor.

◀ This X-ray shows the long, thin bones of the hand and fingers.

▼ A doctor uses a blood pressure cuff to check how well blood is travelling around a patient's body.

X-RAY VISION

When people fall and hurt themselves, they sometimes need to go to a hospital or clinic to have an X-ray to check for broken bones. X-rays can travel through the soft tissue of the body, such as skin and muscles, but not through bones. The X-ray machine sends the X-rays towards the part of the body being examined. A camera on the other side records the rays that travel all the way through the body. The areas where the rays are blocked by bone appear as a white shadow.

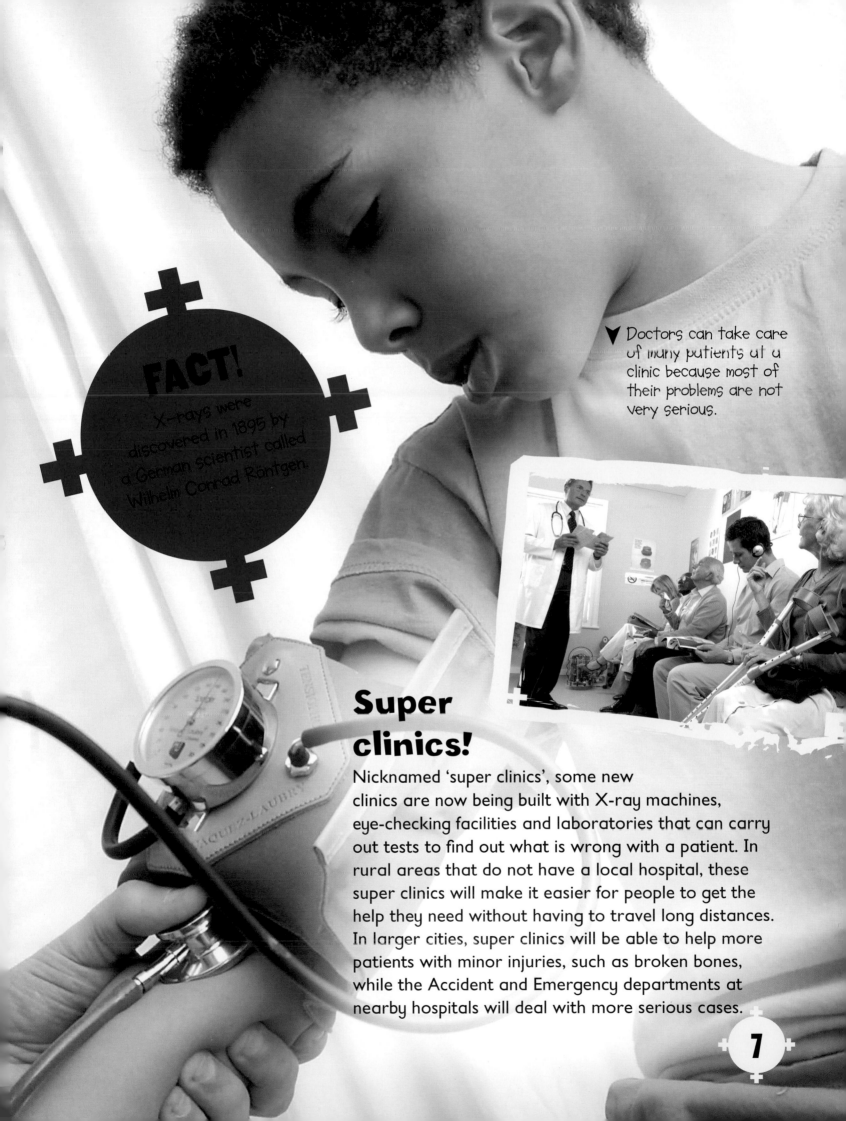

▼ Doctors can take care of many patients at a clinic because most of their problems are not very serious.

Super clinics!

Nicknamed 'super clinics', some new clinics are now being built with X-ray machines, eye-checking facilities and laboratories that can carry out tests to find out what is wrong with a patient. In rural areas that do not have a local hospital, these super clinics will make it easier for people to get the help they need without having to travel long distances. In larger cities, super clinics will be able to help more patients with minor injuries, such as broken bones, while the Accident and Emergency departments at nearby hospitals will deal with more serious cases.

GENERAL HOSPITALS

A general hospital offers treatment for a wide variety of injuries and illnesses. General hospitals have wards and rooms for patients who need to stay in the hospital overnight, storage areas, waiting rooms, **consultation rooms** and a kitchen, where meals are cooked for the patients. Extra-large lifts have doorways wide enough for patients' trolleys. Patients whose injuries or illnesses need to be seen by a doctor immediately go to the hospital's Accident and Emergency department, called A&E. People who dial 999 are usually taken to the hospital A&E department in an ambulance.

▲ People preparing meals in the kitchen wear face masks and gloves to keep germs from getting into the food.

HOSPITAL FOOD

A hospital's kitchen must make thousands of meals a day for its patients, many of whom may be on special diets. Lots of hospitals are trying to use local, **organic** ingredients and new recipes to make their food healthier and more tasty. Some hospitals have menus so that patients can order the meals that they would like to eat.

CAT Scan

A CT scanner, often called a CAT scan machine, is a large machine that uses X-rays to create a three-dimensional (3-D) image of the inside of a patient's body. The CT machine is usually kept in a special **radiology room** which keeps the machine cool enough so that it does not overheat. The patient lies down on a bench, which slowly slides into a large, round hole in the machine, like going into a tunnel. An X-ray beam rotates around the edge of the hole, taking X-rays of the patient from many different angles. The X-rays are then sent to a computer that puts them together to form a 3-D image. This allows the **radiologist** to see details that would have been missed by a traditional 2-D X-ray.

▲ Music is often played to patients while they are inside the CT scanner.

▼ The Accident and Emergency department of a hospital has an **ambulance bay** where emergency workers can bring in patients.

9

EMERGENCY CENTRES

Accident and Emergency departments specialize in taking care of people with severe injuries or who have suddenly been taken ill. An A&E department has a reception area where patients check in and wait with their families. In this area, a **triage** nurse will find out why the patients have come to the emergency department and decide who needs to receive medical attention first. The more serious an injury or illness, the quicker the patient is seen. A nurse will then bring the patient into the emergency ward, which usually has a large, open area with beds that have curtains around them. In some cases, an A&E doctor will be able to **stabilize** the patient using equipment such as **intravenous lines**, medicines or a resuscitation trolley. However, other problems, such as internal bleeding, may require surgery in a different part of the hospital.

HEART BEAT

A resuscitation, or arrest, trolley contains equipment needed when a patient's heart stops beating. The most important machine is the defibrillator, which has two metal-covered paddles that send an electrical charge through the patient's chest to restart the heart. The trolley also carries medicines that help to get the patient's heartbeat back to normal.

▼ Each defibrillator paddle is about the size of a paperback book.

Intensive care

People who have just had serious or life-threatening surgery, or whose bodies cannot perform basic functions, like breathing or eating, are moved to the intensive care unit. Here, specially trained nurses can watch over them day and night. The intensive care unit has **ventilators** that push air into the lungs of patients who cannot breathe on their own. A **gastric feeding tube** can send liquid food directly to a person's stomach if he or she cannot swallow.

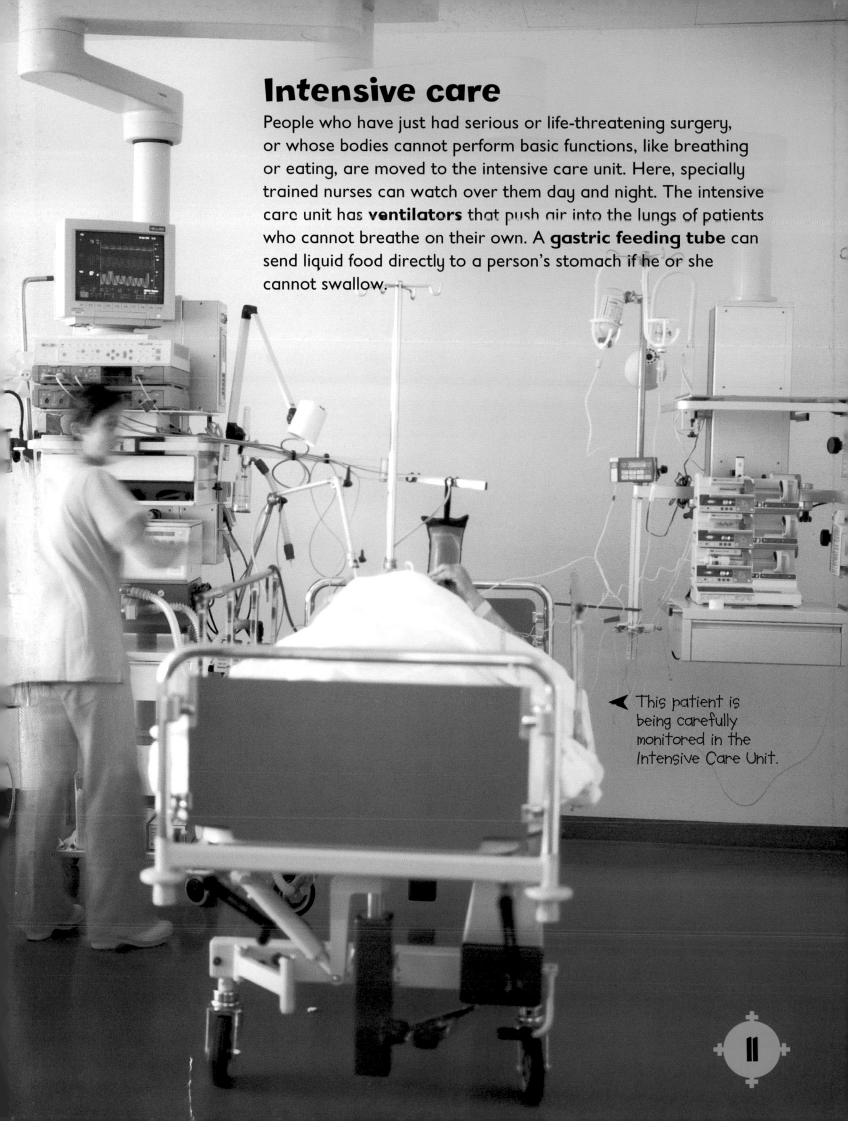

◀ This patient is being carefully monitored in the Intensive Care Unit.

11

TEACHING HOSPITALS

After studying medicine at university, a medical student needs to practise his or her skills on real patients. They do this at a teaching hospital, under close supervision from experienced doctors. The students work in different departments so they can learn about different **specialisms**. Many teaching hospitals also have research areas where doctors can learn about new diseases or try to find cures for existing ones. The research team may ask other doctors to tell them about patients with a particular disease or certain **symptoms** so they can try new types of treatment.

▲ New doctors make **rounds** with a more experienced doctor to see patients and learn more about their illnesses.

Organ transplants

Sometimes, when someone is very ill, they may need one of their **organs** replaced. When this is necessary, surgeons try to find an organ **donor**. The donor must have the same **tissue** and **blood type** as the patient, otherwise the patient's body may reject the new organ. Once a match has been found, the organ is packed in ice and taken as quickly possible to the hospital where the **transplant** surgery will take place. For heart or lung transplants, the surgeons use a heart-lung machine to pump blood around the patient's body to keep all the other organs working during the operation. Once the new heart or lung has been transplanted, the heart-lung machine continues to run until the new organ can work on its own.

▲ This machine adds oxygen to the patient's blood during a transplant operation.

Technicians use a microscope ▶ to compare healthy tissues with diseased ones.

TESTING

Technicians working in a pathology lab **run scientific tests on** bodily fluids **and tissue to find out what is wrong with the patient. A** pathologist **might look at a blood sample to see whether the patient is getting enough iron to stay healthy, or the doctor might examine a piece of tissue under a microscope to look for cancerous cells. In a teaching hospital, the research labs discover as much as they can about new diseases and test new treatments before they are used on patients.**

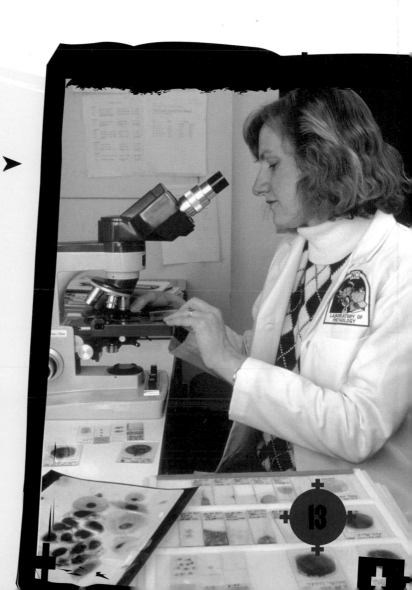

MATERNITY UNITS

Babies are born in the maternity department of a hospital. The mother usually gives birth to the baby in a private room on the **labour** ward. The room has an adjustable bed and machines that can measure the heartbeats of both the mother and baby. After the birth, mother and baby move to the postnatal ward to rest. The baby is placed in a cot beside the mother's bed. Many hospitals also have a birth centre where women are cared for by midwives and can choose to give birth in a water pool.

▲ This newborn baby is being weighed on a special set of scales for babies.

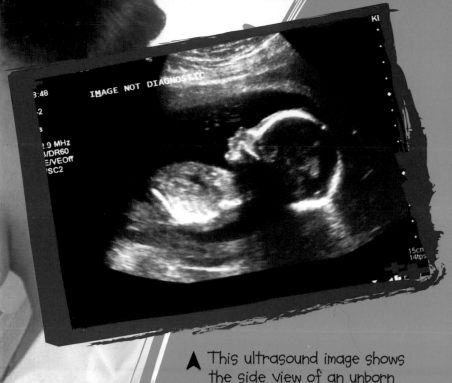

ULTRASOUN MACHINE

Many imaging machines such as X-ray machines and CT scanners can be harmful to babies in the womb, so obstetricians use ultrasound machines to look at unborn babies. A sonographer glides a special hand-held device over the mother's belly which sends out sound waves that cannot be heard by humans. The sound waves travel through the body until they reach an obstacle like an organ. Some of them bounce back to the hand-held scanner while others keep going to the next obstacle. The ultrasound machine measures how long it takes each wave to bounce back and creates a map of the waves that shows the outline of the baby.

▲ This ultrasound image shows the side view of an unborn baby's face and chest.

FACT!
700 000 babies are born in the UK every year!

This **premature** baby is ▶ being bathed by its mother while another baby is kept warm in an incubator.

Keeping babies warm

When babies are born too early, they need medical help to maintain a healthy body temperature. Doctors often put premature babies in a plastic box called an incubator that blows heated air over them to keep them warm. The incubator has several large holes in the sides so nurses or parents can touch the baby without letting out all the warm air. Special blue or white lights may also be used to treat babies who have **jaundice**. This is called phototherapy.

An operating theatre is where surgeons perform operations. The patient lies on an operating table. Bright lamps above the table can be adjusted to provide good lighting during an operation. Machines that monitor the patient's heart rate and breathing and a trolley that holds the surgical instruments are also kept nearby. Cabinets along the walls are full of extra supplies that might be needed.

▼ Everything in an operating room must be completely **sterile** so germs do not get inside the patient's body.

No germs

Germs in an operating theatre can cause life-threatening infections, so surgeons and nurses have to be very careful to keep everything in the operating theatre as clean as possible. Each surgical instrument is disinfected and kept sterile before being used. Surgeons and nurses wear caps over their hair, disposable plastic shoe covers and masks over their noses and mouths. They also carefully wash their arms with special soap before entering the operating room. The water is controlled by a foot pedal and the door swings open and closed so the surgeons do not have to touch any surfaces with their clean hands.

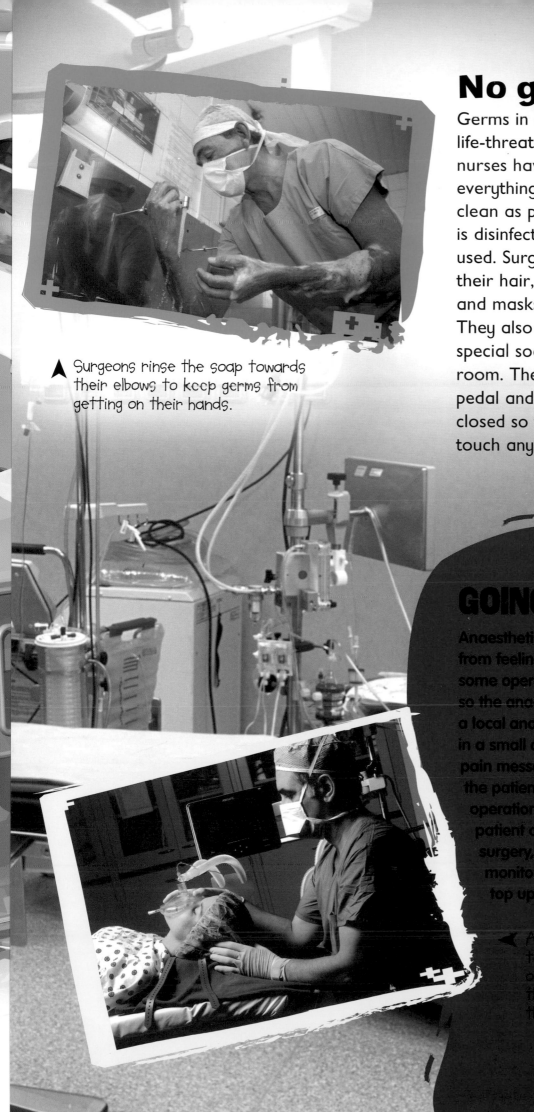

▲ Surgeons rinse the soap towards their elbows to keep germs from getting on their hands.

GOING TO SLEEP

Anaesthetists are doctors that stop patients from feeling pain during an operation. For some operations the patient has to be awake, so the anaesthetist will use a medicine called a local anaesthetic that prevents the nerves in a small area of the body from sending pain messages to the brain. In other cases, the patient needs to be asleep during the operation, so the anaesthetist will give the patient a general anaesthetic. During surgery, the anaesthetist carefully monitors the patient's vital signs to top up the patient's medicine.

◀ Anaesthetic can be given to a patient by injection or as a gas which flows through a mask and puts the patient to sleep.

SPECIALIZED HOSPITALS

General hospitals must be good at taking care of patients with many different illnesses, but some specialized hospitals focus on one type of patient, illness or part of the body. Patients may travel from far away to visit this type of hospital because it has the newest equipment to help them and doctors who have a lot of experience in treating a particular illness. **Oncologists** at a cancer centre, for example, may know about new treatments that can help cancer patients. A surgeon at an eye hospital probably has more experience performing delicate eye surgery than a general surgeon does.

Alberta Children's Hospital

Neonatal intensive care

When premature babies are born with serious health problems that cannot be treated by an incubator, they are often moved to the **neonatal intensive care unit** at a children's hospital. These special nurseries have equipment and medicines that are designed to help babies with **birth defects** such as heart or lung problems. For example, neonatal intensive care units are equipped with machines that can tell how much oxygen is in the baby's blood through a **sensor** taped on the baby's skin, without having to use needles.

▲ This nurse is using a **stethoscope** on a premature baby while giving the baby medicine through a tube.

▼ Many children's hospitals, such as the Alberta Children's Hospital in Canada, are brightly coloured to make them seem less scary to younger patients.

CHILDREN'S HOSPITALS

Doctors at children's hospitals have a lot of experience with the types of diseases that affect growing bodies. They often use smaller versions of medical machines that will fit a child's body better. They may also use toys to make children feel more relaxed and to help them understand what is going on.

◄ After seeing her teddy bear's temperature taken by the doctor, this young girl is not scared to have her own temperature checked.

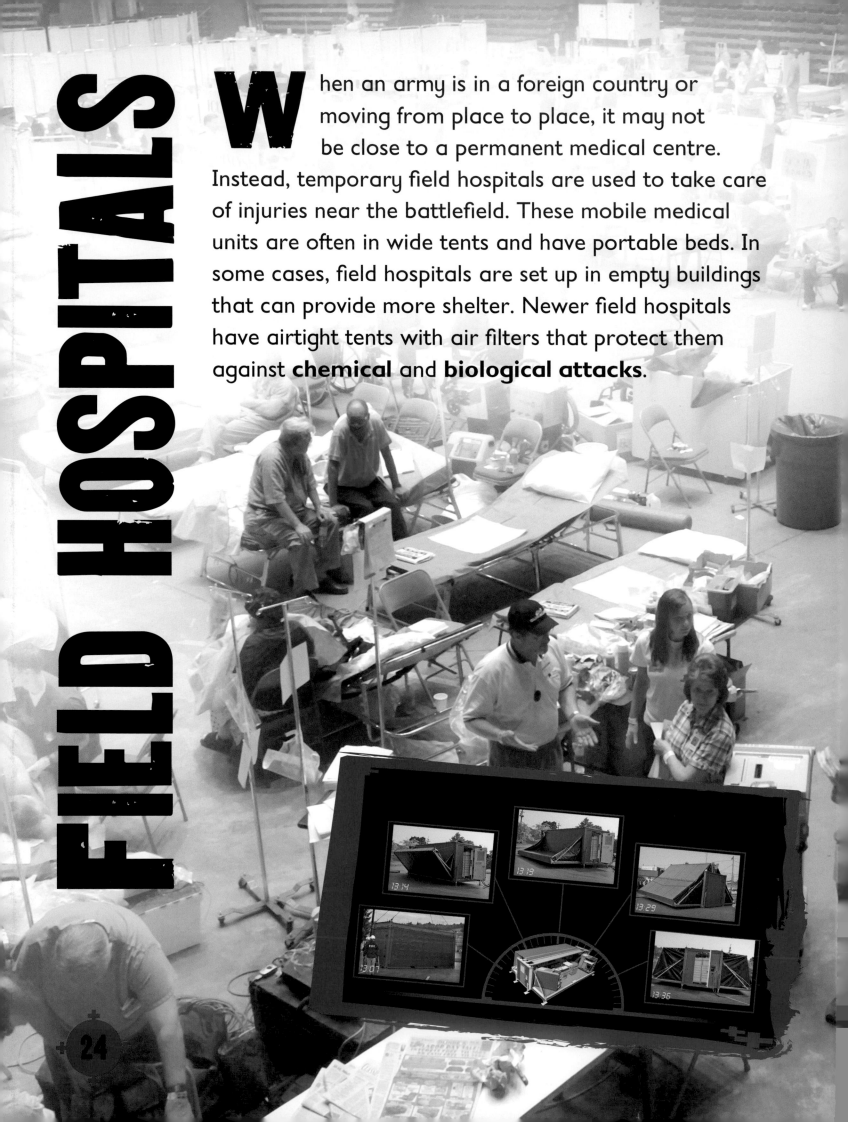

FIELD HOSPITALS

When an army is in a foreign country or moving from place to place, it may not be close to a permanent medical centre. Instead, temporary field hospitals are used to take care of injuries near the battlefield. These mobile medical units are often in wide tents and have portable beds. In some cases, field hospitals are set up in empty buildings that can provide more shelter. Newer field hospitals have airtight tents with air filters that protect them against **chemical** and **biological attacks**.

24

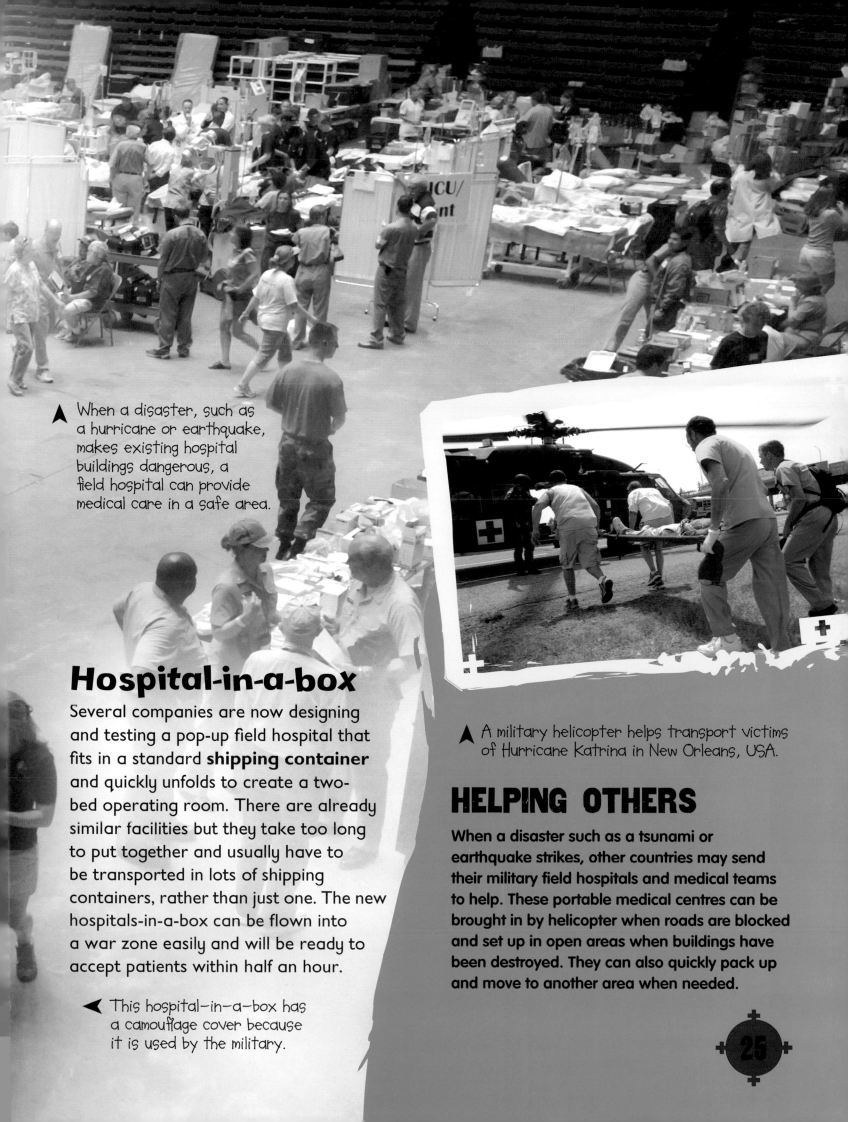

▲ When a disaster, such as a hurricane or earthquake, makes existing hospital buildings dangerous, a field hospital can provide medical care in a safe area.

Hospital-in-a-box

Several companies are now designing and testing a pop-up field hospital that fits in a standard **shipping container** and quickly unfolds to create a two-bed operating room. There are already similar facilities but they take too long to put together and usually have to be transported in lots of shipping containers, rather than just one. The new hospitals-in-a-box can be flown into a war zone easily and will be ready to accept patients within half an hour.

◄ This hospital-in-a-box has a camouflage cover because it is used by the military.

▲ A military helicopter helps transport victims of Hurricane Katrina in New Orleans, USA.

HELPING OTHERS

When a disaster such as a tsunami or earthquake strikes, other countries may send their military field hospitals and medical teams to help. These portable medical centres can be brought in by helicopter when roads are blocked and set up in open areas when buildings have been destroyed. They can also quickly pack up and move to another area when needed.

HOSPITAL SHIPS

Hospital ships are usually large tankers or cargo ships that have been adapted to hold medical facilities such as operating theatres, imaging machines and patient recovery areas. Many hospital ships are used by the military to act as a floating field hospital for soldiers fighting at sea, or in areas where a large land-based field hospital would not be safe. Helicopters are used to bring patients to the ship for treatment, unless the ship is docked at a port. When they are not needed in a war zone, these ships are often sent to disaster areas or poor countries to provide basic health care and surgical facilities for **civilians**. Some charitable organisations also have hospital ships which bring medical help to these areas.

▶ The United States Naval Ship, *Mercy*, is 272.5 metres long and can travel at a top speed of 32.4 kilometers per hour.

FACT!

America's navy ship, *Mercy*, has room for 1000 patients and about 1200 crew members, including doctors, nurses, medical technicians and people to run the ship.

◄ The Royal Fleet Auxiliary ship *Argus* was the British fleet's hospital ship during the Gulf War.

Symbols of peace

Most hospital ships are painted white with large red crosses or crescents to show the enemy that they are not fighting boats and are only working to help look after the injured. However, some hospital ships, such as the *RFA Argus* are not painted with these symbols because they have guns to protect themselves and are also used for other military purposes, such as helicopter training. They are usually called primary casualty receiving ships instead of hospital ships.

BELOW DECKS

Hospital ships have many of the same facilities as a general hospital. The reception area works like the emergency department of a hospital, where patients are examined by a doctor to find out how serious their wounds are. Operating theatres allow surgeons to work in a sterile environment. The ships have supplies for dealing with everything from burns and complicated operations to dental work and making spectacles.

A medical team on duty ▲ aboard the US Naval hospital ship, *Mercy*.

27

HOSPITALS ON WHEELS

When patients cannot get to a hospital because they live in remote areas, or there has been a disaster, the hospital must go to them. Hospitals have used mobile units to bring dental treatment, large imaging machines and women's health centres to rural areas for years. A new pair of travelling hospital trucks used in the USA brings emergency health care to disaster areas. One trailer has walls that can open out to create a full emergency centre and the other is packed with medical supplies.

FACT!

More than 400 000 people have been helped by the hospital train, Lifeline Express, since it started in 1991.

The *Carolinas Med-1* are a pair of trucks based in North Carolina, USA, which carry medical supplies and a working medical centre to disaster areas.

LOOKING INSIDE

A mobile hospital trailer has an operating room with two operating tables and a movable wall which can be used to help keep the operating room sterile and private. The trailer also has four intensive care beds and seven examination tables. A heated and air conditioned tent system can provide as many as 100 beds for additional patients, while a pharmacy provides medicines.

▲ The inside of *Carolinas Med-1* looks very similar to a general hospital's Accident and Emergency department, only smaller.

▼ Machines inside the vision centre of the *Lifeline Express* can check people's vision and make lenses for glasses to help them see better.

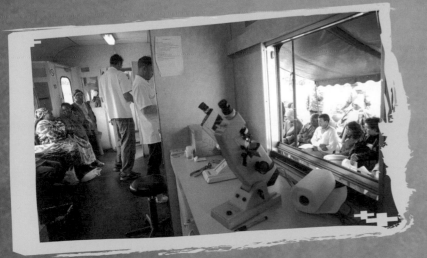

Hospital on rails

Charities in India and Africa have created hospital trains that bring health care to people living in remote areas. The *Lifeline Express* in India was the first hospital train. One of its carriages has been transformed into an operating room with three operating tables and recovery areas. Another carriage has an X-ray machine and tools to check a person's vision. The *Lifeline Express* charity is also planning to transform buses in a similar way, to provide more services to rural areas.

AIR AMBULANCES

An air ambulance is an aircraft such as an aeroplane or a helicopter used to transport very sick or injured people to a hospital. These aircraft usually have **life support** equipment such as a heart monitor, a ventilator to help patients breathe and a defibrillator. Air ambulances have a medical team that may include paramedics, a doctor and a flight nurse, as well as the pilot who flies the aircraft.

▼ Patients are often transported to an air ambulance in a ground ambulance.

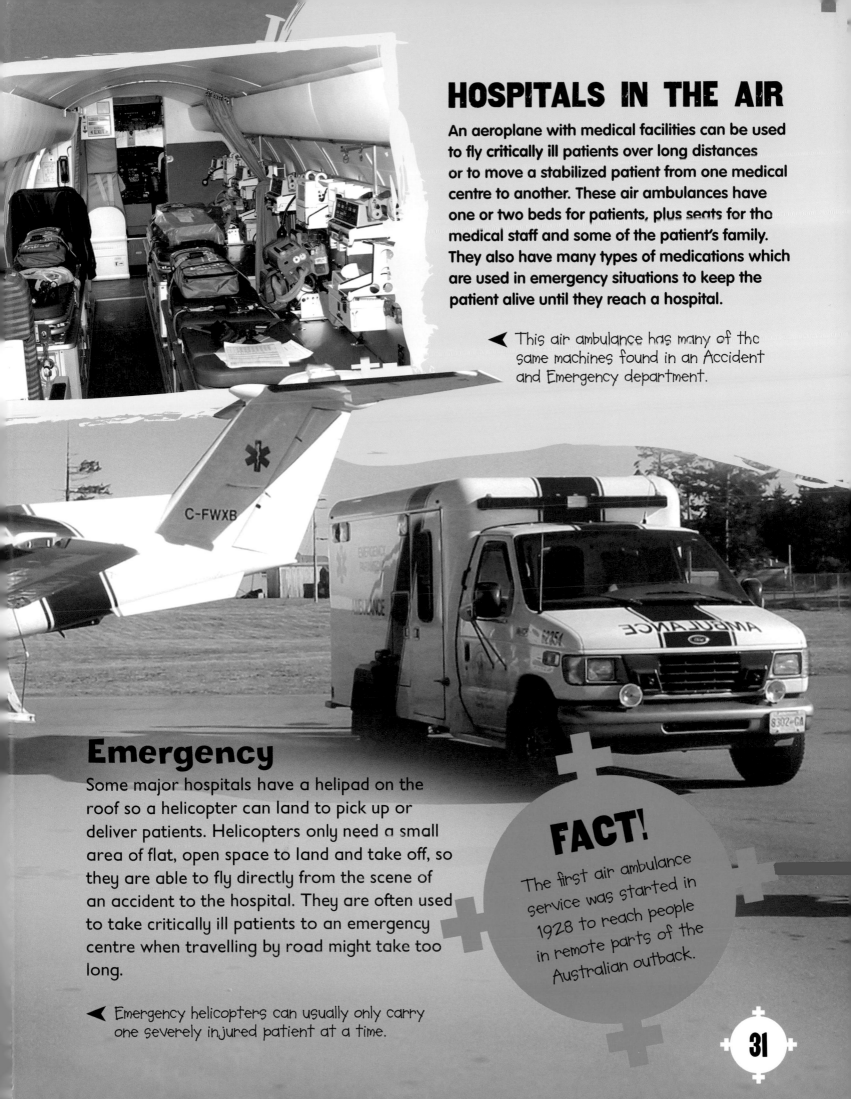

HOSPITALS IN THE AIR

An aeroplane with medical facilities can be used to fly critically ill patients over long distances or to move a stabilized patient from one medical centre to another. These air ambulances have one or two beds for patients, plus seats for the medical staff and some of the patient's family. They also have many types of medications which are used in emergency situations to keep the patient alive until they reach a hospital.

◄ This air ambulance has many of the same machines found in an Accident and Emergency department.

Emergency

Some major hospitals have a helipad on the roof so a helicopter can land to pick up or deliver patients. Helicopters only need a small area of flat, open space to land and take off, so they are able to fly directly from the scene of an accident to the hospital. They are often used to take critically ill patients to an emergency centre when travelling by road might take too long.

◄ Emergency helicopters can usually only carry one severely injured patient at a time.

FACT!

The first air ambulance service was started in 1928 to reach people in remote parts of the Australian outback.

31

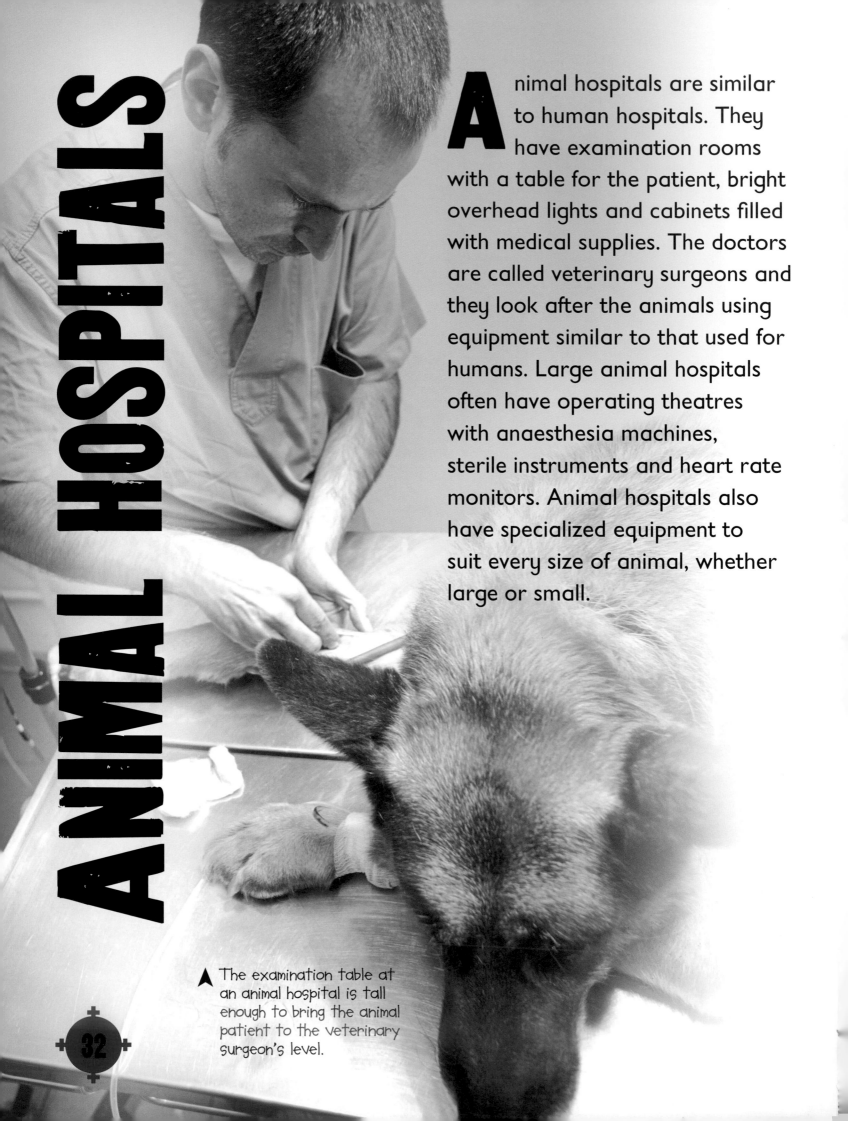

ANIMAL HOSPITALS

Animal hospitals are similar to human hospitals. They have examination rooms with a table for the patient, bright overhead lights and cabinets filled with medical supplies. The doctors are called veterinary surgeons and they look after the animals using equipment similar to that used for humans. Large animal hospitals often have operating theatres with anaesthesia machines, sterile instruments and heart rate monitors. Animal hospitals also have specialized equipment to suit every size of animal, whether large or small.

▲ The examination table at an animal hospital is tall enough to bring the animal patient to the veterinary surgeon's level.

Walking injuries

Animals, especially ones that run a lot such as dogs and horses, often have hip or leg problems. Animal hospitals have special machines to help **diagnose** and treat these injuries. A treadmill is similar to a human exercise machine but with a longer walking surface. It can be used to see how an animal is moving while keeping the animal in one place. Underwater treadmills and large circular pools are often used to help animals who have had leg surgery. Exercise in water can strengthen the animal's leg or hip without putting too much stress on the joint.

▲ The treadmill holds some of the horse's weight so its leg can heal.

GO TO SLEEP

While a doctor can talk to a human patient during an examination and explain what is happening, animals do not understand what is being done to them. Injured animals may try to bite the people who are helping them because they are in pain. Veterinarians often use sedation or general anaesthetic to keep their patients calm.

Just like a human, this lioness is ▲ getting a CAT scan to find out what is wrong with her.

ambulance bay A parking area for ambulances at a hospital.

antenatal care Medical care for a pregnant woman to check she and her growing baby are healthy.

biological attack The use of a weapon containing a very dangerous germ or a natural poison that can harm people.

birth defect A health problem that a person is born with.

blood type There are four different types of blood: A, B, AB and O.

bodily fluids Liquids such as saliva, blood or urine that come from a person's body.

CT scanner An abbreviation for computerized tomography scanner – a machine that creates a three-dimensional image of the body.

chemical attacks The use of a weapon containing dangerous chemicals that can harm people.

civilians People who are not in the military.

clamps Devices for holding something tightly.

consultation room A room where a doctor talks to a patient about the patient's illness and treatment.

diagnose To examine a patient's symptoms and determine what disease or injury is causing them.

donor A person who gives something to someone else.

dressings Something that covers a wound to prevent infection.

gastric feeding tube A plastic pipe inserted into the stomach to give nutrition to patients.

general anaesthetic A substance that stops the body from feeling pain and causes the patient to fall asleep.

imaging machines Machines that show pictures of the inside of a person's body.

intravenous lines Plastic tubes that deliver medicine, nutrition or liquid directly into a patient's blood.

jaundice A disease that makes a patient's skin turn yellow.

labour Giving birth.

life support Machines that help a person perform basic functions, such as breathing.

neonatal intensive care unit A hospital ward where premature or ill newborn babies are monitored and given special medical care.

nurse's station An area from which nurses monitor the patients.

obstetricians Doctors who treat mothers who are pregnant or giving birth.

oncologist A doctor who specializes in treating cancer.

organ Part of the body, such as the heart, liver, lungs and kidneys, that does a particular job.

organic Food that is grown without using pesticides or other chemicals.

out-patients department A unit for treating patients who do not need to be kept in overnight.

paramedics Medics trained to help in emergencies, especially while the patient is being taken to the hospital.

pathologist A doctor who examines bodily fluids and tissues to detect disease.

pathology lab Laboratory where pathologists carry out their tests.

power generator A machine that provides electricity during a power failure.